Terri Jenkin

"Teach what accords with sound doctrine. . .

Teach what is good."

Titus 2:1, 3

Table of Content

Introduction	5
Covered by the Blood	7
Fruit of the Spirit	8
God is Worthy	10
Adventures and Memories	11
Homemaking in the Bible	12
Basis for Happiness	13
Key to Being Blessed	14
Becoming Thankful	15
Belief = Faith	16
Duty need not be a burden	17
Examining the Unspoken	18
Fit for the Master's Use	19
Friend or Foe	20
Friendship	22
God's Boundless Provision	23
God's Landscaping	24
God's Will	25
Plan and Prepare	26
Growing Faith	26
How is your day going?	28
If	29
It's About Him	30
Freedom Guarentee	32
Life of Balance	33
Expression of Love	34
Mentoring through Friendships	36
Spiritual Life Lessons	38
More Life Lessons	39

Mountains and Valley	40
Qualifications for Leadership	41
Respond in Grace	42
Satan's Foothold	43
Examine, Consider and Listen	44
Stress Relief	45
Treasures	46
Walking in the Truth	47
Why Worry—Obey instead	48
We Are Blessed	50
Wings to Fly	51
Desiring Wisdom	52
Finding Wisdom	53
Manifesting Wisdom	54
Women of Encouragement	56
Wonderfully Made	58
Growing Challenges	59
Tired of it or just plain tired	60
Life is Not a Mathematical Equation	61
Only You Can Prevent Forest Fires	62
Falling Stars	63
Sweet Hour of Prayer	65
A Mother's Tribute	66
He Lives	67
The Battle for the Mind	68
Jesus, the Sweetest name	69

For consistency, all scripture is taken from the King James Version

Introduction:

One of my greatest joys is the opportunity to teach, challenge and encourage ladies through the Word of God and from experiences in my own life.

My desire is to share how God strengthens our faith and how, through Christ, we can bear much fruit.

Terri Jenkin

I am crucified with Christ: nevertheless I live; yet not I, but Christ liveth in me; and the life which I now live in the flesh I live by the faith of the Son of God, who loved me and gave himself for me.
Galatians 2:20

Covered by the Blood

In the spring of 2004 our son, Cliff, was diagnosed with Cushing's disease. Throughout the summer his condition worsened. On July 24, he was admitted into Dartmouth Medical Center in NH where he would spend the next six weeks. The bottom line: incurable cancer.

Following those six weeks, he spent two weeks in rehab learning to walk again; then began his first series of Chemo treatments.

Although he had insurance, the remaining expenses to him still amounted to far more than he could pay on his salary as a Christian high school teacher.

The following is an excerpt from my journal during that time:

"We just received letters from two hospitals regarding a financial grant for what the insurance doesn't pay. As I stapled the letter on top of the bills, it reminded me of the debt Christ paid for. Any bills under that letter, we do not owe. Just as any penalty for sin covered under the blood, we do not owe."

"For the wages of sin is death; but the gift of God is eternal life through Jesus Christ our Lord" (Romans 6:23).

"In whom we have redemption through his blood, the forgiveness of sins, according to the riches of his grace" (Ephesians 1:7).

"In whom we have redemption through his blood, even the forgiveness of sins" (Colossians 1:14)

There is a fountain filled with blood

drawn from Immanuel's veins;

And sinners, plunged beneath that flood,

lose all their guilty stains.

Fruit of the Spirit

"But the fruit of the Spirit is love, joy, peace, longsuffering, gentleness, goodness, faith, Meekness, temperance: against such there is no law" (Galatians 5:22-23).

LOVE

"Charity suffereth long, and is kind; charity envieth not; charity vaunteth not itself, is not puffed up, Doth not behave itself unseemly, seeketh not her own, is not easily provoked, thinketh no evil; Rejoiceth not in iniquity, but rejoiceth in the truth; Beareth all things, believeth all things, hopeth all things, endureth all things. Charity never faileth" (1 Corinthians 13:4-8).

The essential ingredient for all the other "fruit" to grow
Love is not a feeling, but a choice

JOY

"And these things write we unto you, that your joy may be full" (1 John 1:4).

A supernatural joy unaffected by people or circumstances

PEACE

"Peace I leave with you, my peace I give unto you: not as the world giveth, give I unto you. Let not your heart be troubled, neither let it be afraid" (John 14:27).

Peace Destroyers: Anxiety and Fear

LONGSUFFERING

" *I . . .beseech you that you walk worthy of the vocation wherewith ye are called, with all lowliness and meekness, with longsuffering, forbearing one another in love"* (Ephesians 4:1-2).

Leave your expectations to God

GENTLENESS

"And the servant of the Lord must not strive; but be gentle unto all men, apt to teach, patient" (2 Timothy 2:24).

Recognize others as being valuable and

must be handled with care

GOODNESS

"Ye shall know them by their fruits. Do men gather grapes of thorns, or figs of thistles? Even so every good tree bringeth forth good fruit; but a corrupt tree bringeth forth evil fruit" (Matthew 7:16-17).

Gentleness involves your attitude,
Goodness involves your action

FAITHFULNESS

"God is faithful. . . "(1 Corinthians 1:9; 10:13)

"Faithful is He. . ."(II Thessalonians 5:24)

"But the Lord is faithful. . ." (II Thessalonians 3:3)

Faithfulness involves being truthful, dependable and loyal

MEEKNESS

"Let nothing be done through strife or vainglory; but in lowliness of mind let each esteem other better than themselves. Look not every man on his own things, but every man also on the things of others" (Philippians 2:3-4).

Meekness means being unselfish

SELF CONTROL

" All things are lawful unto me, but all things are not expedient: all things are lawful for me, but I will not be brought under the power of any" (1 Corinthians 6:12).

Self-Control can simply mean saying no

God is Worthy

God is worthy of our praise and adoration:

The Almighty God is a personal God
"what is the exceeding greatness of His power toward us who believe, according to the working of His mighty power" (Ephesians 1:19).

Without Him, we would be whimpering along the side of the road; instead He has lifted us to our feet and given us solid ground in which to stand—His Word!
"That He would grant you, according to the riches of His glory, to be strengthened with might through His Spirit in the inner man, that Christ may dwell in your hearts through faith; that you, being rooted and grounded in love, may be able to comprehend with all the saints what is the width and length and depth and height — to know the love of Christ which passes knowledge; that you may be filled with all the fullness of God" (Ephesians 3:16-19).

God's mercies strengthen us after great trials as well as during them: He blesses beyond our greatest expectations.
"Now to Him who is able to do exceedingly abundantly above all that we ask or think, according to the power that works in us" (Ephesians 3:20)

He will fulfill all of his promises.
"The LORD will perfect that which concerns me: thy mercy, O LORD, endures for ever: forsake not the works of your hands" (Matthew 28:20).

God does not want us to fear the future; but rather to place our trust in Him and put our confidences in His mercy.
"Peace I leave with you, My peace I give to you; not as the world gives do I give to you. Let not your heart be troubled, neither let it be afraid" (John 14:27).

When God gives us something - whether a blessing or tribulation - it still belongs to Him.

"Every good gift and every perfect gift is from above, and comes down from the Father of lights, with whom there is no variation or shadow of turning" (James 1:17).

And it is <u>always</u> good.

"no good thing will He withhold from those who walk uprightly" (Psalm 84:11).

God allows <u>all</u> things in our lives not to bring conflict, contempt or labor; but to bring forth fruit:

"And not only that, but we also glory in tribulations, knowing that tribulation produces perseverance; and perseverance, character; and character, hope" (Romans 5:3, 4).

Give God your praise and adoration:

"Blessing and glory and wisdom, Thanksgiving and honor and power and might, Be to our God forever and ever" (Revelation 7:12).

Adventures and Memories

There are two famed sayings in our family. Whenever we would venture out into the unknown, we would tell our children; "we're on an **adventure**". So many of these adventures included sleeping in truck stops that our youngest, Clint, once informed us he couldn't sleep unless he heard the sound of a diesel engine.

The other saying "we're making **memories**" would be used when an event was a bit far out like the time my husband, Bill, had us all painting the grout in our kitchen with black shoe polish; [that's a whole story in itself].

My journey as a Christian began in 1973 when I received Christ as my Savior. This journey includes many steps of faith: Moving from Montana to Michigan with two children for my husband to attend Bible College. Moving from Michigan to Florida with four children and establishing four churches. In 2005, we moved back to Michigan, this time with no children to start a new adventure. My husband, Bill, became the President of Continental Baptist Mission.

With these adventures comes memories that are engraved on my mind forever; memories God and I have made together. As believers, we have the wonderful privilege of being on an adventure with a God who is beyond description. Memories along the way are a powerful motivation for believing God in our present and our future.

"I will remember the deeds of the Lord; yes, I will remember your wonders of old. I will ponder all your work, and meditate on your mighty deeds. Your way, O God, is holy. What god is great like our God? You are the God who works wonders; you have made known your might among the peoples" (Psalms 77:11-14).

Take time to recall the adventures and memories you and God have made together. As you remember *"His wonders of old",* may you continue on your journey with great boldness and anticipation of the adventures ahead.

Basis for Happiness

The Beatitudes describe a person blessed by God and living as God intended. The first four Beatitudes focus on our need and are the keys to God's heart. *Blessed are the <u>poor in spirit</u>: for theirs is the kingdom of heaven.*

"Blessed are they <u>that mourn</u>: for they shall be comforted."

"Blessed are the <u>meek</u>: for they shall inherit the earth."

"Blessed are they which <u>do hunger and thirst after righteousness</u>:for they shall be filled." Matthew 5:3-6

- **Poor in Spirit** demonstrates our need for God – *"without me ye can do nothing"* (John 15:5).

- As **mourners** we are made aware of our brokenness and our need for the Holy Spirit of God – *"...the God of all comfort; Who comforteth us in all our tribulation"* (2 Corinthians 1:3-4).

- Being **meek** is submitting to God – *"Take my yoke upon you, and learn of me; for I am meek and lowly in heart: and ye shall find rest unto your souls"* (Matthew 11:29) and realizing as John the Baptist did – *"He must increase, but I must decrease"* (John 3:30).

- **Hungering and thirsting after righteousness** is yearning for spiritual food – *"O God, thou art my God; early will I seek thee: my soul thirsteth for thee, my flesh longeth for thee in a dry and thirsty land, where no water is"* (Psalms 63:1).

If we could just read God's Word and obey it, God would not have to use circumstances in our lives in order for us to recognize our need of Him. It is through such trials that we instinctively turn to God and surrender ourselves totally to Him. He then can mold us and make us into the image of his Son

I trust this is a reminder of what you already know and will encourage each of us to Praise God for His sufficiency to meet our every need.

Key to Being Blessed

The first four beatitudes taught us that through **humility, brokenness, submission** and **yearning for His Word** we recognize our need for God and turn our mind toward Him. Where the first four beatitudes focus on our need, the following five focus on giving.

Each one is a characteristic of Christ which God expects us to demonstrate to the world around us. Matthew 5:7-10

- **Compassion** – *"Blessed are the merciful; for they shall obtain mercy"*- This is outworking of faith to meet the needs of others.

- **Holiness** – *"Blessed are the pure in heart: for they shall see God"*- A lifestyle of set-apartness, both in thoughts and actions.

- **Reconciliation** – *"Blessed are the peacemakers: for they shall be called children of God"*- Forbearance instead of retaliation; forgiveness of wrongs and restoration of fellowship.

- **Commitment** – *"Blessed are they which are persecuted for righteousness' sake: for theirs is the kingdom of heaven"* – Steadfast loyalty that cannot be broken.

- **Patience** – *"Blessed are ye, when men shall revile you, and persecute you, and shall say all manner of evil against you falsely, for my sake"* - Willingness to endure suffering.

As our need for God grows, He gives accordingly to mold and shape us into the image of Christ for the purpose of expressing Himself through us. Martin Luther said "It is the duty of every Christian to be Christ to his neighbor."

Are there qualities in your life He is working on? Ask Him to give you opportunities to 'flesh" them out –

You will be **Blessed!**

Becoming Thankful

*"As you therefore have received Christ Jesus the Lord, so walk in Him, rooted and built up in Him and established in the faith, as you have been taught, **abounding in it with thanksgiving**"* (Colossians 2:6-7).

"Roots are unseen" – No one sees our private time with God; the time we spend nourishing yourself through His Word. *"Thou art my hiding place and my shield: I hope in thy word"* (Psalms 119:114).

"Roots are for taking in" – the Word of God supplies us with the necessary spiritual food for daily living. *" All scripture is given by inspiration of God, and is profitable for doctrine, for reproof, for correction, for instruction in righteousness: That the man of God may be perfect, thoroughly furnished unto all good works"* (2 Timothy 3:16-17).

"Roots are for storage" – When difficulties come, God's Word will sustain us and lift us above our circumstances. *"Thy word is a lamp unto my feet, and a light unto my path"* (Psalms 119:105).

Be *rooted and built up in Him*: Spend time in the Word and give Jesus Christ priority in your life:

The results will be –

You will not be shaken by the events in your life,
your life will be characterized by goodness, righteousness and truth,
you will be a thankful person!

Belief = Faith

One of my New Year resolutions was to grow in my knowledge of God. Since I was would be home for several months, I took the opportunity to be involved in three different Bible studies:

The common thread of the three studies was believing God.
→Believing that God is in absolute control and nothing happens outside His watchful eye.
→Believing God's Word is truth.
→Believing God does not lie, He does not change His mind, and what He says He will do--He will do; His Word is trustworthy *"God is not a man, that he should lie. . .Hath he said, and shall he not do it? Or hath he spoken, and shall he not make it good?"* (Numbers 23:19).

We can believe God and trust Him for our eternal destiny, yet fail to find Him trustworthy in our day to day challenges. Every step forward we take with God, we take through faith. When we hit an unexpected obstacle in our path or a dip in the road; we can fall, lay on the side of the road whimpering; or we can pick ourselves up, dust ourselves off and go forward. Worries and doubts do not need to overtake us when we trust in God's promises.

When confronted by circumstances we simply cannot understand, we must trust in God. *"Trust in the LORD with all thine heart; and lean not unto thine own understanding. In all thy ways acknowledge him, and he shall direct thy paths"* Proverbs 3:5-6.

"The LORD will perfect that which concerneth me: thy mercy, O LORD, endureth for ever" (Psalms 138:8)

The Lord God of heaven and earth, the One who created all things and holds the universe in His hand; He is our Shepherd, who cares and keeps us as a shepherd cares and keeps his sheep.

Cultivate this relationship and watch our faith grow.

Duty need not be a burden

The mark of a woman who is living according to God's plan is that she enters each tomorrow with great excitement and enthusiasm.

Duty is something we ought to do as a Child of God: " *our duty to do"* (Luke 17:10), *"duty to minister"* (Romans 15:27), *"fulfilled my duty to God"* (Acts 23:1).

The list of duties as God's servants are numerous. In my personal life, my duties include being a helpmeet to Bill: doing all things to allow him to do what God has called him to do.

God warns us that it is possible for our duty as a servant to become a **burden** – *"be not weary in well doing"* (2 Thessalonians 3:1; Galatians 6:9)*; "run and not be weary"* (Isaiah 40:31).

Burden can mean simply a responsibility or obligation; but it also means a weight. In itself it is not bad; it is our allowing a task or service to become a weight; pulling us down. God does not intend for our service to become a burden; "*For it seemed good to the Holy Ghost, and to us, to lay upon you no greater burden than these necessary things"* (Acts 15:28).

"Take my yoke upon you . . . and ye shall find rest; for my yoke is easy, and my burden is light (Matthew 11:29). God is not saying to place the burden on him, but to place our care and anxiety on him. When we are yoked together with Christ; His power and strength is ours.

When we allow circumstances or people to burden us down, it is because we truly do not believe God is powerful enough. My favorite preacher always says: What we believe determines how we act; *"For as he thinketh in his heart, so is he" (*Proverbs 23:7).

I trust I have given you something to think on. It should be our desire to enter each day with great excitement and enthusiasm; and if we don't, we need to evaluate why according to the truth of God's Word.

Examining the Unspoken

Are you familiar with the saying, Actions speak louder than words? How about: Actions speak instead of words? You're probably thinking; I've never heard that one before and you're right. That's because I just made it up, but we've been doing it for years.

Nonverbal communication can play a huge roll in getting a negative point across: folding of the arms, turning of the head, and we've all experienced the rolling of the eyes. On the other hand, it can also convey the joy of the LORD in our life.

Nonverbal communication can convey. On a recent trip, I observed the pastor's wife and came to the conclusion that she did not enjoy being a pastor's wife. Her nonverbal communication conveyed frustration and unhappiness. Later, as we visited, she shared many disappointments and concerns which she unknowingly was conveying through her outward expressions.

We serve a WONDERFUL and GLORIOUS GOD! We may not always have the chance to verbally share Christ with others, but we **always** have the opportunity to communicate His influence in our lives. *"Let your light so shine before men , that they may see your good works, and glorify your Father which is in heaven"* (Matthew 5:16).

Be encouraged: *"greater is He that is in you, than he that is in the world"* (I John 4:4).

Therefore, *"the joy of the Lord is your strength"* (Nehemiah 8:10).

My challenge to myself and to you is: Do unbelievers see your relationship with the Lord as worth having?

Fit for the Master's Use

True Faith has to do with our relationship with God; not what we do, but who we are. We are children of God; people who live close to Him. We must do our best to keep that relationship right and healthy.

We focus on diet, exercise, and medicine to keep ourselves physically and mentally healthy. But what about keeping our relationship with God healthy?

- **Diet**: As believers, the Holy Spirit lives in us. Are we eating junk food or healthy food? What you feed the Holy Spirit will weaken the old nature and what you feed the old nature will weaken the Holy Spirit. Since we should all be far enough along in our Christian walk to know the difference, I will leave it up to each of us to personalize it and make changes where changes are needed.

- **Exercise**: Serving the Lord is great exercise! Just don't forget to stretch yourself. Remember physically, we have to lift that extra weight if we are to go beyond our capabilities. Keep in mind, however, that 'over exercising' can cause injury.

  The key is balance.

- **Medicine**: *"If we say that we have no sin, we deceive ourselves, and the truth is not in us. If we confess our sins, he is faithful and just to forgive us our sins, and to cleanse us from all unrighteousness"* (1 John 1:6-9).

God's medicine for a healthy relationship with Him works. If we make a mistake, we need to fix it, because our relationship with God will suffer. This medicine is called *"confession of sin."* The first sip is admitting we did wrong, the second sip is to tell God we are sorry, and the third sip is to yield ourselves to God anew.

We have the opportunity to put our time, energy and talent into something that is worthwhile—a life with God. This is a life that will never end; blessings and joys that last forever. Stay healthy so you can live your life as God planned it.

Friend or Foe

"Ye are my friends, if ye do whatsoever I command you"
(John 15:14)

Like Abraham, we can be called a friend of God. *John 15:4* tells us how we can do whatever He commands us--Ab*ide in Him.*

Abiding in Him requires:

Absolute Faith

> *"As you therefore have received Christ Jesus the Lord, so walk in Him, rooted and built up in Him and established in the faith"* (Colossians 2:6-7). We received him by Faith; we must live by faith--going forward without knowing the outcome; trusting God for who He is.

Godliness

> Godliness is not just an action but an attitude toward God. *"Whatsoever ye eat or drink, or whatever you do, do all to the glory of God"* (I Corinthians 10:31). Paul tells Timothy in *1 Timothy 4:7 exercise thyself rather unto godliness.* Godliness is developed through an intimate relationship with God. It means denying old desires, ways, practices, and habit patterns; daily saying no to self and yes to Christ until one by one all the old habitual ways are replaced by new ones. *"**put off** concerning . . . the old man, And . . . **put on** the new man, which after God is created in righteousness and true holiness"* (Ephesians 4:24).

Consecration:

> Consecration is something God has done---He has set us apart for HIS USE. *"Ye have not chosen me, but I have chosen you"* (John 15:16).

Absolute Abandonment:

It is our human responsibility to surrender our whole being to God—spirit, soul and body, In order for a lump of clay to be made into a beautiful vessel, it must be **entirely abandoned** to the potter. *"Hath not the potter power over the clay"* (Romans 9:21). We must place ourselves in God's hands without any reservations.

Simple Obedience.

Obedience involves following Christ ". . . *follow me"* (Luke 9:23).

Find fellow believers who are willing to follow Him. *". . . whosoever therefore will be a friend of the world is the enemy of God"* (James 4:4).

As it is in all areas of our Christian life; the choice is ours.

Friendship

"A man who has friends must himself be friendly, but there is a friend who sticks closer than a brother" (Proverbs 18:24).

Jesus had many acquaintances, but He knew that good friends must be chosen carefully. Jesus shared his heart on a more intimate level with three men in particular: Peter, James and John. They were the ones chosen to be with Jesus at the transfiguration and during His final hours in the Garden of Gethsemane.

We have in our lives these same levels of friendship. Acquaintances are folks we come in contact with during day to day living. We should not take them lightly as God has instructed us to show Christ to whoever we meet along the way; *"You are the light of the world"* (Matthew 5:14). Friends are the ones who are likeminded on issues that matter and with whom we have things in common. Finally there are those good friends with whom we have cultivated a deeper relationship. *"A man that hath friends must shew himself friendly: and there is a friend that sticketh closer than a brother"* (Proverbs 18:24).

Years ago, after praying for a special friend for our daughter, Debby, God brought another MK to the Christian school our children attended. Debby and Anne became best friends, encouraging and admonishing each other to grow spiritually.

Throughout our ministry, I have had numerous acquaintances, both saved and unsaved. I count as my friends those who labored with us during the planting of our four churches, other pastors' wives, and missionary wives. Among these friends, there are those I can count on without reservation; the ones who rejoice with me in spiritual victories and who pray with me during spiritual battles.

May God bring into your lives friends who will encourage you, admonish you to grow spiritually, and be there when you need that special hug!

God's Boundless Provision

Our person, possessions, and position in life are reliant upon God.

WE ARE WHO WE ARE BECAUSE OF GOD.

"I will praise thee; for I am fearfully and wonderfully made: marvelous are thy works; and that my soul knoweth right well" (Psalms 139:14).

WE HAVE WHAT WE HAVE BECAUSE GOD HAS SEEN FIT TO GIVE IT TO US.

Who makes you different from others? What do you have that *"you did not receive? If then you receive it, why do you boast as if you did not receive it?"* (1 Corinthians 4:7)

WE HAVE THE PRIVILEGE OF SERVING HIM BECAUSE IT PLEASES HIM.

"But now hath God set the members every one of them in the body, as it hath pleased him" (1 Corinthians 12:18).

WE MUST USE WHAT GOD HAS GIVEN US WISELY IN ORDER TO SERVE HIM EFFECTIVELY.

The emphasis of Paul's prayer for the Ephesians is spiritual understanding and authentic Christian character. He does not ask God to give them what they do not have, but rather he prays that God will reveal to them what they already possess. Our responsibility is to apply our knowledge of Him in order to love Him more, experience His victory in all things and regard His wisdom above all else.

May we recognize and appreciate God's unlimited generosity and never forget that all we have comes from HIM—*"...that ye may be perfect and entire, lacking nothing"* (James 1:4).

God's Landscaping

When we arrived home after being on the road for six weeks, I was delighted to see a green lawn and my flowers in full bloom. Looking closer, however, I saw weeds had sprung up throughout the landscaping.

As I began the tedious work of removing these weeds; I found some came out pretty easy while others had embedded themselves deep into the ground and after grabbing hold and pulling with all my might, a gaping hole was left in its place. Weeds are a lot like sin in our life. Dealt with daily, they never have a chance to take root; however, when left alone, they not only take root but multiply. *"The cares of this world and the deceitfulness of riches choke the word"* (Matthew 13:22).

Down the slope on the east side of the house, I planted ground cover with the hope it would eventually eliminate our need to mow. Unlike weeds, grass is good, but I did not want it in that particular area. Likewise in our lives; just because something is good, it doesn't necessarily mean it's the best for us. *"All things are lawful for me, but all things are not expedient: all things are lawful for me, but all things edify not"* (1 Corinthians 10:23).

All the weeding and keeping the grass out of where it doesn't belong wouldn't make a difference if I didn't regularly water and fertilize. This is absolutely necessary if the landscaping is going to be healthy and beautiful. In our spiritual life we must feed upon God's Word if we are to have a healthy and productive Christian walk for others to look upon. *"Having your conversation honest among the Gentiles: that, whereas they speak against you as evildoers, they may by your good works, which they shall behold, glorify God in the day of visitation"* (1 Peter 2:12).

Be sure and give thanks to Him who enables us-- through His Word, His Grace and His Power-- to be in His Word, to keep a clean slate before Him and to make the right choices so we can be productive vibrant Christians. *"According as his divine power hath given unto us all things that pertain unto life and godliness, through the knowledge of him that hath called us to glory and virtue"* (2 Peter 1:3).

God's Will

"And be not conformed to this world: but be ye transformed by the renewing of your mind, that ye may prove what is that good, and acceptable, and perfect, will of God" (Romans 12:2).

Last month, our son, Cliff's new mother-in-law pulled me aside during the wedding reception and said, "Isn't it wonderful to know our children are in the center of God's perfect will?"

This comment got me thinking about my desire to be right where God wants me to be and doing exactly what God wants me to.

Have you discovered wanting God's will in your life and doing it are two different things? Our heart and mind say yes, but so many times our actions say no. Speaking from personal experience, aligning my life with Him can become difficult when it comes in conflict with what I want to do. So many times, my actions are self-motivated—that is to say, what will benefit me or what is most comfortable for me.

God's Will doesn't always give us all the facts and details up front (and I am a facts-n-details kind of person!), yet He never fails to take care of details. While saying "yes" may mean sacrifices (and a few surprises); it will always mean bountiful blessings.

Cliff and Megan don't have all the details of their future (Cliff was diagnose with incurable cancer in 2004), and there have been and will be many sacrifices, yet God's plan and purpose will be accomplished.

What has God been asking you to do? Does it seem impossible? Do you feel He has chosen the wrong person? Are you listing reasons you can't rather than the ways He can?

"Not with eyeservice, as menpleasers; but as the servants of Christ, doing the will of God from the heart" (Ephesians 6:6).

May the Holy Spirit be the encourager as you walk by faith according to the Word of God!

Plan and Prepare

While planning a recent trip; I checked the internet for the best deals, purchased airline tickets and made hotel reservations. It needed special attention because I was making my way to Oklahoma then on to meet up with my husband, Bill, to help a missionary family survey Northwest Arkansas. I needed to look ahead, choose wisely and take steps to bring it together.

I was also planning and organizing a ladies' day retreat. After bathing it in prayer; a theme was chosen, a speaker secured, workshops were formulated and publicity sent out to some area churches. But then, I found myself prying into the future—poking my nose in where it doesn't belong—asking questions like: What if only a few ladies come? What if too many ladies come? The anticipation of the day was becoming a burden.

I knew that fretting over the outcome was a waste of my time and energy. It was serving no purpose except to cloud the excitement of the day. *"Take therefore no thought for the morrow: for the morrow shall take thought for the things of itself. Sufficient unto the day is the evil thereof"* (Matthew 6:34)

We should plan and prepare, but we need not concern ourselves with the outcome. God has a way of weaving all of our past experiences, relationships and connections into a life plan that we could never have figured out on our own.

I trust this has been a reminder to change your 'what if' to 'whatever' and rest in Him. We can then look to the future with great expectation to what He is going to accomplish.

"Call unto me, and I will answer thee, and show thee great and mighty things, which thou knowest not" (Jeremiah 3:33).

Growing Faith

Some time ago, I was given a miniature rose bush. Since we keep our house pretty cool in the winter, I thought it would be best if the plant made its home in Bill's office where the temperature and light were more suitable for growing. Bill nearly killed it with neglect, so fellow worker stepped in to rescue it. He just recently returned it to me complete with a delicate blooming rose.

Likewise, Faith needs nurturing to develop and yield fruit.

- God provides the proper soil for our faith to take root. *"He shall be like a tree planted by the river of waters"* (Psalms 1:3).

- He showers us with the right amount of blessings and trials to produce growth. *"the trying of your faith worketh patience but let patience have her perfect work, that ye may be perfect and entire, wanting nothing"* (James 1:3).

- He places us where we will best mature; sometimes in the midst of others for stability. *"For if they fall, the one will lift up his fellow"* (Ecclesiastics 4:10).

God is patient as He waters, nurtures, and prunes our faith until we "bloom" for all to see. " *. . and I will show thee my faith by my works"* (James 2:18).

This does not leave us without responsibility to do what we can to grow a greater faith.

Listening to what He has to say; Keeping our eyes on Jesus;

Thinking about God's goodness, mercy, power and love;

Talking about the goodness of God,

Witnessing to the lost and Serving others.

This Divine/human cooperative in growing a greater faith will result in lives of trustworthiness, integrity, fidelity, passion, loyalty, dependability, consistency, courage and strength.

Live according to His Word, and grow in your faith every day that you live.

How is your day going?

Are you accomplishing what you set out to do when you woke up this morning? I love it when I get up, go down stairs, pour a cup of coffee and head to my devotion nook. I read, study, pray and meditate. Wow! My day is going great. My focus is on the Lord.

This morning, I got up and could hardly move without my back screaming at me. My coffee wasn't ready; so I headed back upstairs to shower and get ready to volunteer at the office. I hate to leave the bed unmade, so I quickly threw it together. By the time I was dressed and ready, Bill had breakfast made and was headed off to the office. Before he left he offered to get my phone for me so I didn't have to run up the stairs again.

Now I needed to make my lunch, pack up my basket of items to take to the office, let Leah out to do her business and put her bed & food in the car (she spends the day with me at the office). Now; how's my day going? I'm late; I don't have enough hands to carry it all in one trip, and I can't find my phone (it finally dawned on me that Bill probably had it, and he did).

Pulling out of the driveway I heard a clunk. Oh-oh, my coffee mug was left on top of the car when I put Leah in her carrier. There was my coffee spread across the road. I took a deep breath and used the drive time to refocus—not on me and my morning—but on the Lord and what He had for me today.

May I challenge you as I was challenged a short time ago: What we choose to focus on will make a world of difference in how our day progresses. Be Christ focused and not self-focused!

"Thou wilt keep him in perfect peace, whose mind is stayed on Thee" (Isaiah 26:3).

"A merry heart maketh a cheerful countenance: but by sorrow of the heart the spirit is broken" (Proverbs 15:13).

"A merry heart doeth good like a medicine: but a broken spirit drieth the bones" (Proverbs 17.22).

If . . .

"If my people, which are called by my name, shall humble themselves, and pray, and seek my face, and turn from their wicked ways; then will I hear from heaven, and will forgive their sin, and will heal their land" (2 Chronicles 7:14)

Although written specifically to the Israelites; the principle can be applied to us as children of God.

#1 <u>Humble</u> <u>ourselves.</u> While the Old Testament understanding of humility includes lowliness, the New Testament meaning is primarily a personal dependence on God. It doesn't come naturally since we are full of pride. *"He hath shewed strength with his arm; he hath scattered the proud in the imagination of their hearts. He hath put down the mighty from their seats, and exalted them of low degree"* (Luke 1:51-52).

#2 <u>Pray.</u> *"Search me, O God, and know my heart: try me, and know my thoughts: And see if there be any wicked way in me, and lead me in the way everlasting"* (Psalms 139:23-24).

#3 <u>Seek</u> <u>His</u> <u>face.</u> This means to search out who God is and strive after what He wants. This, too, is an unnatural action. We would rather seek enjoyment, entertainment, and prosperity. *"For all seek their own, not the things which are Jesus Christ's"* (Philippians 2:21).

#4 <u>Turn</u> <u>from</u> <u>our wicked</u> <u>ways.</u> This requires a decision and an action of turning back or retreating from a specific course of life. *"That ye put off concerning the former conversation the old man, which is corrupt according to the deceitful lusts"* (Ephesians 4:22).

Although this was written specifically to the Israelites; the principle can be applied to us personally as children of God.

"Humble yourselves" (James 4:10); *"pray"* (1 Thessalonians 5:17); *"seek His face"* (Luke 11:9); and *"turn from your wicked ways* (2 Timothy 3:4-5). God can then work through us and through the church to make an impact on the country.

Recognize God is still in control, and His mercy and grace are at work in your life today.

It's About Him

"To keep me from becoming conceited because of the surpassingly great revelations there was given me a thorn in the flesh, a messenger of Satan, to torment me" (2 Corinthians 12:7).

Preachers and commentaries teach that Paul's 'thorn in the flesh' was most likely bad eye sight based on *"What large letters I use"* (Galatians 6:11).

God gave a 'thorn' to Paul so it would not be Paul's greatness but God's message that had preeminence. Since thorn in the Greek means a bodily annoyance or disability, there could be other possibilities:

> • **Carnality**
> *"What I want to do, I do not do; but what I hate, I do"* (Romans 7:14)
>
> • **Adversary hindering him**
> *"Alexander did me a great deal of harm"* (2 Timothy 4:14)
>
> • **Bodily affliction**
> *"in person he is unimpressive* (2 Corinthians 10:10)
> *"in my infirmities"* (2 Corinthians 12:5)
>
> • **Defective speech**
> *"his speaking amounts to nothing"* (2 Corinthians 10:10)
> *"not in excelling of speech"* (1 Corinthians 2:1)

Any of these could also be 'thorns' in our life. God allows them so we will not rely on our own abilities; nor should we use them as excuses.

> • **Carnality**: do not allow present or past sins to hinder us. *"lay aside every weight, and the sin which doth so easily beset us"* (Hebrews 12:1).
>
> • **Adversary**: Satan doesn't want us to serve God in any way and will use individuals to discourage us through criticism or mocking; *"Be sober, be vigilant; because your adversary the devil, as a roaring lion, walketh about, seeking whom he may devour"* (1 Peter 5:8).

• **Bodily affliction**: Many, if not all of us, have some type of physical difficulty which we could use to tell God; "I can't". *"I can do all things through Christ which strengtheneth me"* (Philippians 4:13).

• **Defective speech**: We are not all great speakers. I personally have a speech impediment and could use that as an excuse just as Moses did. *"I am slow of speech and slow of tongue"*. God said: *"go, and I will be with your mouth and teach you what you shall say"* (Exodus 4:10).

May we understand God's *"grace is sufficient. . .His strength is made perfect in weakness";* so we, like Paul, can say; *"I will glory in my infirmities, that the power of Christ may rest upon me"* (2 Corinthians 12:9).

It's not about us—it's about HIM!

Freedom Guarentee

"Declare His glory among the nations, His marvelous deeds among all people" (Psalms 96:3).

I just returned from three weeks with my daughter, Debby, and our grandchildren in Germany. Besides giving Debby a break from the 24/7 care of the kids, we enjoyed visiting Christmas markets in Cologne and Munich as well as Strasbourg, France.

Debby lives on the German economy (not on the Military base) and has a decoder box attached to her TV which provides American programs through the Armed Forces Network Europe. The commercials are educational and patriotic. One AFN commercial was "Name the Capital"; another one gave information about former presidents. Did you know that Andrew Jackson was once the governor of Florida? After living in Florida for 20 years, I did not know that. I know you're thinking the same thing I did—"Oh yeah, of course, Jacksonville."

My favorite was "Reaching out from Home" where families of each deployed company send a message to their soldier in Iraq. Different ones played throughout the day, and my grandchildren would always check to see if it was "their" commercial.

The families of those fighting in Iraq would love to have their soldier home, but they also knew that they were giving the Iraqis the hope of freedom and a prosperous life.

As Christians we have more than the hope of freedom, we have a guarantee of freedom—*"Therefore if the Son makes you free, you shall be free indeed"* (John 8:36); and we have a prosperity that goes beyond material possessions—*"According as his divine power hath given unto us all things that pertain unto life and godliness"* (2 Peter 1:3).

Declare His **glory** and His **marvelous deeds** that guarantees your eternal freedom.

Life of Balance

Sometimes our life is a whirlwind of roles and responsibilities. Recently my daughter, Debby, in Germany told me of the day she carefully planned in detail only to have Sydney become ill. What mom has not had a day disrupted by a sick child or worst yet, mom wake up with a headache and sore throat. How do we respond to interruptions? Are we quick to say; "not now Lord, I have things to do" or "OK Lord, what do YOU have for me today"?

When we are self-centered (what I expect and want to do) and not God-centered (what does He have for me today?), our life is off balance. An off balanced life is exhausting and spiritually unfruitful because it depends on self-power, not on God's power. *"For it is God which worketh in you both to will and to do of his good pleasure"* (Philippians 2:13)

Our God is a God of balance, and even in our daily schedule; He wants us to be balanced. Yes, we plan; yet, we do so with the idea that God may have something different for us, He may have some good works for us to walk in, or He may give us some interruptions causing us to be challenged spiritually, or He simply may want us to refocus.

"Lord you are my chosen portion and my cup; you hold my lot. Indeed, I have a beautiful inheritance. I have set the Lord always before me; because he is at my right hand, I shall not be shaken. Therefore my heart is glad, and my whole being rejoices. My flesh also dwells secure. You make known to me the Path of Life. In your presence there is fullness of joy. At your right hand are pleasures forevermore" (Psalms 16:5, 6, 8, 9, 11).

Begin each day in prayerful dependence on God. Recognize that your life comes to you day by day, hour by hour directly from the hand of God. Daily evaluate your focus, your purpose and your dependency upon God.

Expression of Love

How do you express your love to the special ones in your life: Red hearts, stuffed animals, valentine cards, diamonds? Many years ago on Valentine Day, the announcement of Bill and my engagement appeared in the newspaper encased in a heart. Two unsaved 18 year olds getting married based on a limited knowledge of love. Looking back, I realize we had no idea the kind of commitment love required. Statistic would show that our marriage had a minimal chance of surviving. Having a child in the first year lessened those chances even more.

Praise the Lord for our salvation so early in our marriage. However, even after accepting Jesus Christ as our Savior, we still had to learn what love really was (and we continue to learn). But now we have an instruction book, the Word, and a guide, the Holy Spirit to teach us.

1 Corinthians 13:4-7

'Charity suffereth long, and is kind; [but what about those irritating habits],

charity envieth not; [yes, but he always gets to . . . and I never],

charity vaunteth not itself, is not puffed up, [if it wasn't for me . . .],

Doth not behave itself unseemly, seeketh not her own, [if we don't get to go or do that . . . I'm not going to be happy—and if momma ain't happy, nobody's happy].

is not easily provoked, thinketh no evil; [You are always doing and and if you don't stop that, I am going to. . .].

Rejoiceth not in iniquity, [I have no sympathy for you; you reap what you sow] *but rejoiceth in the truth;*

Beareth all things, believeth all things, hopeth all things, endureth all things." [If you love someone, you will be loyal to him no matter what the cost. You will always believe in him, always expect the best of him, and always stand your ground in defending him.]

Although these are familiar verses; I know from experience there are circumstances every day and sometimes several times a day which will test the application of them.

My challenge for you is to make a conscience effort to put into practice the Love that God has shed abroad in your hearts.

"And hope maketh not ashamed; because the love of God is shed abroad in our hearts by the Holy Ghost which is given unto us" (Romans 5:5).

Mentoring through Friendships

To Be an Effective Mentor we must be a friend worth having:

- **Have the goal to please God** - *2 Corinthians 5:9*
- **Be a listener** - *James 1:19*
- **Be a learner** - *Proverbs 18:15*
- **Be patient** - *Proverbs 14:29*
- **Be cheerful, not a complainer** - *Proverbs 15:31*
- **Don't be quarrelsome** - *2 Timothy 2:24.*
- **Be gentle** - *Philippians 4:5*
- **Be dependable** - *Proverbs 25:19*
- **Be kind, compassionate and forgiving** - *Ephesians 4:32*
- **Be honest** - *Ephesians 4:25*
- **Be sensitive** - *Proverbs 25:20 - Proverbs 27:14*
- **Build up others. Be an encourager** - *Ephesians 4:29*
- **Be submissive to authority** - *Proverbs 13:13*
- **Don't be pushy** - *Proverbs 25:17*
- **Be polite** - *I Corinthians 13:5*

To be an effective Mentor, we must be willing to give of our time, energy and resources with one instruction:

- **Be discerning**

  Discernment means to judge closely or examine carefully. Discernment is essential for knowing when, where, and how we're to give to others; it guides us in recognizing true needs. *Ecclesiastics 8:5-6*

God is our source for discernment and wisdom. He is the one who gives us eyes to see and hearts to understand the needs around us.

We need to learn two important tasks together: giving and guarding. Learn to give openly and freely to others while guarding ourselves from committing to people and things that God has not called us to.

Four questions to ask ourselves:

1. Will it really help this person?

2. Have I sought God's direction?

3. What is my motive for helping?

4. Is this what I'm supposed to do right now?

As a mentor and friend, the greatest thing we can do is point them to the one who can truly meet their deepest needs.

Spiritual Life Lessons

I used to watch TLC's Trading Spaces, What Not to Wear, and Flip that House during which they advertise **TLC's Life Lessons** such as: Not everything comes back in style; When you're a mom, there is no rest room; When buying a new house, save some money for new drapes; or Know when not to do it yourself.

Likewise, as I have sat under my husband's preaching for over 33 years, there are some **Spiritual Life Lessons** that are etched in my mind.

#1 **Do the right thing whether you feel like it or not.** *"Therefore to him that knoweth to do good, and doeth it not, to him it is sin"* (James 4:17). Feelings can be very deceiving. I don't always feel like reading the Bible or praying or going to church or being kind to those who hurt me. I don't always feel pleasant and cheerful. Have you noticed, as I have, that when you do the right thing, your feelings follow?

#2 **If you neglect the Word of God, you will fail.** It may not be a great catastrophic failure, but rather, simply not having the spiritual victories God intends for me and you to experience. *"Study to shew thyself approved unto God, a workman that needeth not to be ashamed, rightly dividing the word of truth"* (2 Timothy 2:15).

#3 **You are as close to God as you want to be.** The choice is ours. *"Know ye not, that to whom ye yield yourselves servants to obey, his servants ye are to whom ye obey; whether of sin unto death, or of obedience unto righteousness"* (Romans 6:16)? It is easy to be close to God during difficulties, but it is more of a challenge when things are going smoothly.

More Life Lessons

I recently heard a Christian say; "Satan took his life"; speaking of a faithful servant who was doing great things for God. This quickly brought to mind three **Life Lessons** from Bill's teachings that are embedded in my mind. Not only have they carried me along during difficult times, but they also help me during small unexpected bumps in the road.

#1 Our God is not tied up in a corner while Satan is having a heyday with us. Do not give Satan undeserved credit for difficulties in our life. Satan may know our habits and can place obstacles in our path, but he cannot harm God's children beyond what God allows. *"When thou passest through the waters, I will be with thee; and through the rivers, they shall not overflow thee: when thou walkest through the fire, thou shalt not be burned; neither shall the flame kindle upon thee"* (Isaiah 43:2).

#2 The same circumstances which God would use to make us stronger more effective Christians, Satan would use to trip us up and cause us to be ineffective for Jesus Christ. It is not God, but rather us who allows Satan to have a victory in our lives. *"My brethren, count it all joy when ye fall into divers temptations; Knowing this, that the trying of your faith worketh patience. But let patience have her perfect work, that ye may be perfect and entire, wanting nothing"* (James 1:2-4).

#3 God could have prevented it, but He didn't because he wants to make us more like His Son, Jesus Christ. *"But he knoweth the way that I take: when he hath tried me, I shall come forth as gold"* (Job 23:10).

Great confidence comes with knowing God is in absolute control and knowing He wants only the best for His children.

Mountains and Valleys

Are "mountains" when we are high with excitement and expectation, or are they the challenges we face?

Are the "valleys" when we are low and can't see our way out, or are they the times when all is calm beside the still waters? Either way you look at it, God wants us to have the victory.

Some look at challenges with excitement and great expectation for what God is going to do. For others, the challenges stop us in our tracks because our strength wanes and it seems insurmountable.

Right before Christmas, our son-in-law's stepmother passed away after a battle with cancer. Dan returned from Iraq, met up with Debby and the kids in Germany, and flew to Florida. God provided and I flew down for a weekend to see all four of our grandchildren—an exciting mountain experience.

When I returned home, I was down (oops, am I supposed to admit that?). Couldn't I just pull myself up by the boot straps (an old western adage) and snap out of it? No, but the Holy Spirit through God's Word could: *"For the LORD God is a sun and shield; The LORD will give grace and glory; No good thing will He withhold from those who walk uprightly. O LORD of hosts, blessed is the man who trusts in You!"* (Psalms 84:11-12) I was able to refocus just as David did in Psalms 13:1 *"How long will thou forget me . . ."* vv. 5 & 6 *"But I have trusted in thy mercy; my heart shall rejoice in thy salvation. I will sing unto the Lord, because He hath dealt bountifully with me."*

I saw with more clarity how God fulfills His joy in us. He wants our joy to be full, but when circumstances seem contrary to that, He allows us to experience Him. He renews us with His Spirit. Yes, He may change our circumstances, but then again, He may not. In the end the choice was ours.

Choose to thank Him, praise Him, and live joyfully in His presence!

Qualifications for Leadership

As a missionary, it is necessary to wear many hats in the process of planting a church.

I just returned from Germany where I had the privilege to visit Dan and Debby's church. The Sunday I was there, they had a guest speaker. He made the following statement: "A leader is one who knows the way, goes the way and shows the way."

We must **know the way** to salvation.

> *"I am the way, the truth, and the life: no man cometh unto the Father, but by me"* (John 14:6).

We also need to **know the way** to a successful Christian life.

> *"Master, we know that thou art true, and teachest the way of God in truth"* (Matthew 22:16).

> *"This man was instructed in the way of the Lord; and being fervent in the spirit, he spake and taught diligently the things of the Lord . .."* (Acts 18:25).

Knowing the way, we must then **go the way.** This involves our walk, talk, actions, and our reactions.

> *"But as he which hath called you is holy, so be ye holy in all manner of conversation"* (1 Peter 1:15).

Knowing the way and going the way, we must out of necessity **show the way.**

> *"Ye are the light of the world. A city that is set on an hill cannot be hid. Neither do men light a candle, and put it under a bushel, but on a candlestick; and it giveth light unto all that are in the house. Let your light so shine before men, that they may see your good works, and glorify your Father which is in heaven"* (Matthew 5:14-16).

My challenge to you is simple: **KNOW THE WAY, GO THE WAY**, and **SHOW THE WAY** so that our Father in heaven will be glorified.

Respond in Grace

The biblical definition of *worketh* is **energy** which gives a clarity to how God enables us to respond in grace.

God will give us **energy** do his good pleasure; the **energy** to be perfect in Christ Jesus.

> *"For it is God which worketh in you both to will and to do of his good pleasure"* (Philippians 2:13).

It is God's **energy** that works in us MIGHTILY.

> *"Whom we preach, warning every man, and teaching every man in all wisdom; that we may present every man perfect in Christ Jesus: Whereunto I also labour, striving according to his working, which worketh in me mightily"* (Colossians 1:28-29).

The same **energy** that worked in Christ to raise Him from the dead is the same power that **energizes** us to live a victorious Christian life. Just stop and think on that. How powerful is your God? Our God is powerful enough to raise Jesus Christ from the dead! And that same power is available to me and to you as children of God.

> *"And what is the exceeding greatness of his power to us-ward who believe, according to the working of his mighty power, Which he wrought in Christ, when he raised him from the dead, and set him at his own right hand in the heavenly places. . ."* (Ephesians 1:19-20).

The working of grace in our lives enables us to respond—not with fear, anger or bitterness but with kindness, peace and forgiveness.

Whatever God has allowed in our life—the uncertainty of our economy, personal finances, an illness, a death in the family, difficult people and/or circumstances—are all opportunities for us to grow and respond in Grace.

Be encouraged!   What God has asked of us He also gives us *"energy"* to do it.

Satan's Foothold

Why were God's people not able to get away from their unfaithfulness, disobedience and sinful nature after they settled in the Promised Land?

When the Israelites conquered and then settled in the Promised Land, they had not followed **all** of God's instructions. They allowed those who did not worship the living God of Israel to live among them. The influence of these idolaters was greater than the influence of God's people.

God's instruction to us may not be the exact words He spoke to the Israelites when they went in to conquer the land, but His Word is still clear:

> *"Be ye **not unequally yoked together with unbelievers**: for what fellowship hath righteousness with unrighteousness? and what communion hath light with darkness?. . ."*
>
> *Wherefore **come out from among them, and be ye separate**, saith the Lord, and **touch not the unclean thing**; and I will receive you,"* (2 Corinthians 6:14,17).
>
> *"But as he which hath called you is holy, so **be ye holy** in all manner of conversation; Because it is written, **Be ye holy**; for I am holy"* (1 Peter 1:15-16).

We need to be challenged: to evaluate what we allow **as an influence** [power, pressure, authority, control] in our life.

What we allow in our life **to influence** [persuade, manipulate, induce, sway, change, inspire, shape] our decisions and actions?

Simply---are there areas where Satan can get a foothold? If the answer is yes, now is the time to make those changes in obedience to God's Word.

Examine, Consider and Listen

My grandson, Stetson, received a green helium balloon at his church's fall festival. The following day, he wanted us to untie it from the pumpkin serving as an anchor. His mom calmly told him what would happen if it was untied, and if he did not hang on to it, it would rise to the ceiling out of his reach. Stetson was certain he wanted it untied; so she went on to explain he was making a choice, and if it did go up, he could not whine or cry about it. He said, as you would expect a three year old to say; "OK I won't."

Later that day while taking the dogs out, Stetson followed with his balloon in hand. I suggested he take it back in the house so he wouldn't lose it. He assured me he had it secure in his hand; but less than a minute later, off it went. Up, Up, Up. I looked at Stetson's face as it began to crinkle up into a cry. I said compassionately; "remember what your mom said; it was your choice." He looked at me and responding calmly; "I'm so upset my balloon flew away." That was it. No crying, no whining. When his dad and mom returned home he told them; "I'm so upset my balloon flew away." I was impressed with his basic understanding of choices and consequences.

There is always a cost to choices we make. Therefore, we should exercise wisdom when faced with a decision.

#1 Examine the situation. .

#2 Consider the whole picture instead of our own narrow view.

#3 Listen more than you talk. *"let every man be swift to hear, slow to speak, slow to wrath"* (James 1:19). Sometimes listening will help us know what not to do. *"So that you incline your ear to wisdom, and apply your heart to understanding;"* (Proverbs 2:2).

#4 Take a second look in light of the wisdom God gives. God's wisdom sometimes goes against what we want to do since our emotions cause impulsive responses. *"Consider what I say, and may the Lord give you understanding in all things"* (2 Timothy 2:7).

I trust this has given you, as it did me, something to ponder as you face new and exciting adventures.

Stress Relief

Stress! My life would be so much simpler if I could eliminate it completely.

Stress is **tension within** created when we perceive that our needs or desires are not going to be met. Although it varies according to each of our personalities and situations there are certain catalysts for stress: fatigue, both physically and emotionally; pride and an independence "I can do it" attitude; time restrains and expectations, whether ones we place on ourselves or ones placed on us by other people.

On a Sunday morning in Montana while working at the cabin, **I** was getting breakfast for everyone, and **I** didn't have time to take a shower or fix my hair before leaving for church. Questions were being asked that **I** needed to answer; things needed to be done that **I** needed to do.

Although some of the circumstances were out of my control, my response was not. Frustrated I thought; why not skip Sunday school? After all, Bill wasn't teaching. The Holy Spirit rebuked me; **NO-- you do the right thing whether you feel like it or not!!** We did go, and the pastor's sermon was Thriving in Times of Stress.

Managing stress begins with understanding our strengths and weaknesses and knowing what Scripture teaches about the nature of God. God has allowed circumstances into my life which cause chaos knowing it will give me opportunities to grow more like His Son, Jesus Christ.

> *"Search me, O God, and know my heart; try me, and know my anxieties; and see if there is any wicked way in me, and lead me in the way everlasting"* (Psalms 139:23, 24).

Are there things we can do to help eliminate stress in our lives? We can get the rest we need, delegate responsibility, stop procrastinating, and place our expectations on God for He is the only one who can meet them.

> *". . .let us lay aside every weight, and the sin which so easily ensnares us, and let us run with endurance the race that is set before us, looking unto Jesus, the author and finisher of our faith"* (Hebrews 12:2).

TREASURES

The first chapter of Ephesians is packed with nuggets of treasure which should excite us when it comes to recognizing who we are in Christ.

But first, Paul reminds us of who we were: Ephesians 2:1-3

- unable to understand spiritual things or do anything spiritual to please God;
- living according to the world's standards and with the world's values;
- allowing Satan to have an active influence in our lives by causing us to doubt and question God's Word.

From this he proclaims the treasurers that are ours:

- **God made us alive in Christ!** *(Ephesians 2:5)*
- God the Father has **chosen us** and **made us heirs** to His Kingdom *(Ephesians 1:4, 5).*
- Through Christ we have been **forgiven and redeemed** *(Ephesians 1:7).*
- The Father has given the **Holy Spirit as an earnest** to guarantee His promises will be kept, and He has **sealed us** unto the day of redemption. He will finish His work and bring us to glory *(Ephesians 1:13, 14).*
- **Every blessing of the Spirit is ours;** everything we need for a successful satisfying Christian life *(Ephesians 1:17-19).*

I trust you are getting a glimpse of the "treasure" that is ours through salvation. I also want to remind us that these riches are the basis for our life and power as we serve Him. *Ephesians 2:10* tells us *"we are His workmanship* [poem of God / expression of God] *and* He has *ordained* [already prepared] *good works for us to walk in."*

"Dig in" for yourself and find the nuggets of treasure that He has for you in His Word.

Walking in the Truth

Bill would often gently tell our kids "use your head". That was his way of saying; think it through, evaluate it, stretch yourselves mentally and come up with an answer.

God does not simply hand us all the answer, but He has given us His word, the basis for our faith – *"I will instruct you and teach you in the way you should go"* (Psalms 32:8), and He has given us the Holy Spirit – *"But the Helper, the Holy Spirit . . . will teach you all things, and bring to your remembrance all that I said"* (John 14:26).

As parents, we believed it was important to teach our children to make choices—friendships, jobs, obedience toward authorities—based on the truth of God's Word and **not** on their feelings, circumstances or pressures from the outside. *"How can a young man keep his way pure? By living it according to your word"* (Psalms 119:9).

I have heard people say; "But God would . . ." or "God wouldn't want . . ." even when they know God's Word says differently. *"And do not be conformed to this world, but be transformed by the renewing of your mind, so that you may prove what the will of God is, that which is good and acceptable and perfect"* (Romans 12:2).

Not only do they mold themselves after the world, but they want to mold God along with them so that He fits into their lifestyle and decisions. *"If we say that we have fellowship with Him, and walk in darkness, we lie and do not practice the truth"* (I John 1:6).

It is essential that we search God's Word and think biblically so we will evaluate our thoughts, considerations and decisions against the Truths of God's Word; *"Be diligent to present yourself approved to God, a worker who does not need to be ashamed, rightly dividing the word of truth"* (2 Timothy 2:15).

As physical parents and as spiritual parents, we have the responsibility to teach that God's Word is the final authority, and Truth does not change with circumstances; *"The entirety of Your word is truth, and every one of Your righteous judgments endures forever"* (Psalms 119:160).

Why Worry—Obey instead!

♫ Obedience is the very best way to show that you believe. ♪ Doing exactly what the Lord commands; doing it happily... ♫ Action is the key, do it immediately, joy you will receive. ♪ Obedience is the very best way to show that you believe.♪ ♫

- Don't worry about your life

  "...take no thought of your life" (Matthew 6:25)

- Don't worry about tomorrow

  "Take no thought for the morrow..." (Matthew 6:34)

- Don't worry about anything

  "Be careful for nothing..." (Philippians 4:6)

- If you have worry, throw it all on Him

  "Cast all your care upon him" (1 Peter 5:7)

You may say; "I don't worry, but . . . there are things that stress me out." I challenge you to stop and ask yourself: "WHY? Where is God?"

Some of you are saying to me, "I know all that, but I worry because it is important to me." You may even say, "You have no idea what I'm facing."

Let me assure you – **I have been there!**

A few verses that have made the biggest impact on my life in the area of worry are:

> *"He will keep you in perfect peace, whose mind is stayed on Thee [Him]"* (Isaiah 26:3).

How do you keep your mind "stayed on him" when you are tempted to worry or get stressed out?

> *"Finally, brethren, whatever is true, whatever is noble, whatever is right, whatever is pure, whatever is lovely, whatever is admirable –if anything is excellent or praiseworthy—think about such things"* (Philippians 4:8).

What is TRUE? –

"The Lord will renew our strength" (Isaiah 40:31)

"The Lord will perfect what concerns us" (Psalms 138:8)

" The Lord is our shield" (Proverbs 30:5)

"The Lord will sustain us" (Jeremiah 17:8)

"all things work together for good to them that love God, to them who are the called according to his purpose" (Romans 8:28)

"greater is He who is in us than he who is in the world" (1 John 4:4)

The best thing you can say about worry is that it is

> worthless
>
> wasteful,
>
> wicked.

God has better things for you to do and greater victories for you to experience than stressing out over areas of which He has complete control.

♫ Action is the key, do it immediately, ♫ JOY you will receive.♪

We Are Blessed

"The Lord bless you and keep you" (Numbers 6:24). These are the first words of the benediction God commanded Aaron to pronounce upon the people of Israel.

A recent word study brought to light the multilayered meaning to this word.

We are blessed people; not because of what God gives us, but because of who God is and who we are in Him. The word "blessed" which appears in the Beatitudes *(Matthew 5:3-11)* is many times translated 'happy'. However it is much deeper than simply being happy; it is the inner joy and contentedness <u>not</u> based on physical or temporary circumstances. *"Not that I speak in respect of want: for I have learned, in whatsoever state I am, therewith to be content"* (Philippians 4:11).

It is "happiness" based on our position before God. Our sins have been forgiven, put out of sight <u>never</u> to be held against us. A Greek scholar refers to blessed as "the state of being marked by fullness from God. *"Blessed are they whose iniquities are forgiven, and whose sins are covered. Blessed is the man to whom the Lord will not impute sin"* (Romans 4:7-8).

The very core of this word "blessed" is that we have become a partaker of God's nature; in knowledge, righteousness, and holiness. *"Whereby are given unto us exceeding great and precious promises: that by these ye might be partakers of the divine nature,"* (2 Peter 1:4).

God has also promised personal blessings to those who follow Him in obedience. *"Blessed is the man that endureth temptation: for when he is tried, he shall receive the crown of life, which the Lord hath promised to them that love him"* (James 1:12).

Even though this past year has brought great pain and sorrow, I can give thanks for being truly blessed and look with great anticipation to how God is going to bless my life as I continue to grow and yield my life to Him.

May God set you apart for His Glory, and may you experience the blessedness that only God can give you.

Wings to Fly

"But those who wait on the LORD shall renew their strength; they shall mount up with wings like eagles, they shall run and not be weary, they shall walk and not faint" (Isaiah 40:31).

Wait on the LORD.

Wings of complete surrender and Wings of absolute trust are available to us in order to escape from all that can hurt and trouble us. *" but will with the temptation also make a way to escape, that ye may be able to bear it"* (1 Corinthians 10:13).

His wings will carry us into the life *"hid with Christ in God"* (Colossians 3:3).

When I face a mountain of difficulties, my tendency is to work hard and try to tunnel my way through causing myself great frustration, or I try to find my own way around it. My own self sufficiency and doubt hinder me while God's desire is for me to fly over it 'in His Power'.

> *"He found him in a desert land and in the wasteland, a howling wilderness; He encircled him, He instructed him, He kept him as the apple of His eye.*
>
> *As an eagle stirs up its nest, Hovers over its young, Spreading out its wings, taking them up, carrying them on its wings, so the LORD alone led him, and there was no foreign god with him. "He made him ride in the heights of the earth"* (Deuteronomy 32:10-13).

Many years ago, we read to our children about the eagle pushing its young out of the nest in order to teach them to fly. God does the same with us. When we face trials we need to view them in the light of our wings being developed.

When God stirs up your comfortable nest and pushes you over the edge, my challenge is to surrender yourself totally and place your trust in the one who can make you FLY.

Wisdom: Part One—Desiring Wisdom

My desire to grow in the knowledge of our Lord is incomplete without also desiring wisdom. Knowledge is the start of our relationship with Him; Wisdom develops this relationship into a living and vibrant one. Wisdom is more precious than anything else we can desire.

> *"Happy is the man that findeth wisdom, and the man that getteth understanding. For the merchandise of it is better than the merchandise of silver, and the gain thereof than fine gold. She is more precious than rubies: and all the things thou canst desire are not to be compared unto her"* (Proverbs 3:13-15).

Wisdom is an acquired skill of applying knowledge.

When there were decisions to be made regarding Cliff's medical needs, we prayed that God would give the doctors wisdom. At a crucial time, the chief of the medical staff entered the picture. He had knowledge of the extreme degree of Cushing disease that plagued Cliff. He applied that knowledge and made the decision to remove Cliff's adrenal glands rather than the cancer tumors. He made the right choice according to his knowledge.

Wisdom will:

→direct us to walk in the way that is both true and good.

→protect us on the path He has set for us.

→lead to sound, wise action and speech.

→enable us to see the big picture, keep our cool, form a plan and effectively influence others.

→allow us to live a life that is pleasing to God.

"When wisdom entereth into thine heart . . . thou mayest walk in the way of good men, and keep the paths of the righteous" (Proverbs 2:10 & 20).

I trust you desire a life that is characterized by wisdom!

Wisdom: Part two: Finding Wisdom

God granted Solomon his greatest desire; wisdom. *"Give me now wisdom and knowledge. . ."* (2 Chronicles 1:10).

James tells us we too can ask God for wisdom, and He will give it to us. *"If any of you lack wisdom , let him ask of God. . . and it shall be given him"* (James 1:5).

In my study of wisdom, I have found three means by which we can obtain wisdom. Although each one is valuable in itself, "finding wisdom" involves their union.

- His Word: *"Study to shew thyself approved unto God, a workman that needeth not to be ashamed, rightly dividing the word of truth"* (2 Timothy 2:15).

- The Holy Spirit: *"B*ut God hath revealed them unto us by his Spirit: for the Spirit searcheth all things, yea, the deep things of God. For what man knoweth* [capability to understand] *the things of a man, save the spirit of man which is in him? even so the things of God knoweth* [ability to draw conclusion based on knowledge] *no man, but the Spirit of God. Now we have received, not the spirit of the world, but the spirit which is of God; that we might know* [experience the things of God]*the things that are freely given to us of God"* (1 Corinthians 2:10-12).

- Godly men and women who have seen God's truth in action: *"A wise man will hear, and will increase learning; and a man of understanding shall attain unto wise counsels"* (Proverbs 1:5).

"For this reason, since the day we heard about you, we have not stopped praying for you and asking God to fill you with the knowledge of his will through all spiritual wisdom and understanding. And we pray this in order that you may live a life worthy of the Lord and may please him in every way: bearing fruit in every good work, growing in the knowledge of God" (Colossians1:9-10).

Wisdom: Part Three: Manifesting Wisdom.

We cannot flip a switch to obtain wisdom, and in order to manifest wisdom in our lives; we must become Biblical thinkers.

WWJD (what would Jesus do) was extremely popular a few years back. It was embraced not only by believers but the unsaved who created a Jesus that accommodated their own desires. We know true wisdom is properly framed in a living relationship with the Lord; *"Who is a wise man and endued with knowledge among you? Let him shew out of a good conversation his works with meekness of wisdom"* (James 3:13).

The following is not an exclusive list of the characteristics of a wise person, but I trust will wet your appetite for further study.

- **Separated:** *"When wisdom entereth into thine heart, and knowledge is pleasant unto thy soul; Discretion shall preserve thee, understanding shall keep thee: To deliver thee from the way of the evil man, from the man that speaketh forward things; That thou mayest walk in the way of good men, and keep the paths of the righteous"* (Proverbs 2:10-12; 20)

- **Used of God:** *"But God hath chosen the foolish things of the world to confound the wise; and God hath chosen the weak things of the world to confound the things which are mighty"* (1 Corinthians 1:27).

- **Pure, Peace-loving, considerate, submissive, full of mercy and good fruit, impartial and sincere**: *"But the wisdom that is from above is first pure, then peaceable, gentle, and easy to be entreated, full of mercy and good fruits, without partiality, and without hypocrisy"* (James 3:17).

- **Humble:** **"***When pride cometh, then cometh shame: but with the lowly is wisdom"* (Proverbs 11:2).

- **Stable:** *"And wisdom and knowledge shall be the stability of thy times, and strength of salvation: the fear of the LORD is his treasure"* (Isaiah 33:6).

- **Sharing Christ:** *"Walk in wisdom toward them that are without, redeeming the time. Let your speech be always with grace, seasoned with salt, that ye may know how ye ought to answer every man"* (Colossians 4:5-6).

None of us knows the number of days we have to serve the Lord. May we seek wisdom so we will use each and every day for the God's glory. *"So teach us to number our days, that we may apply our hearts unto wisdom"* (Psalms 90:12).

Women of Encouragement

Webster's definition of **communication** is *"an exchange of ideas and information by speech, gestures, or writing."* This short study of Scripture will give us a taste of God's definition, and how we can use communication as either a means of encouragement or discouragement. The choice is up to us.

Communicating though words is powerful.

James 3:1-13 gives us many truths regarding the tongue and the power of it.

- Do not use your words to judge or censure others.
- Controlling our tongue is proof that we are mature Christians in that we also have control over our actions.
- An unruly tongue is one of the greatest evils.
- It is very difficult to control our tongue (without supernatural grace and assistance.)
- Our tongue can be used in the service of God if we so choose.

Ephesians 4:25-32 instructs us as to what type of words we are to speak.

- Words of Truth.
- Not angry words.
- Words of encouragement and healing.
- Kind words.
- Words of forgiveness.
- Speak with a purpose and with a great deal of caution.

Communication through listening. *"Swift to hear, slow to speak"* (James 1:20).

"He that is void of wisdom despiseth his neighbour: but a man of understanding holdeth his peace" (Proverbs 11:12).

"He that answereth a matter before he heareth it, it is folly and shame unto him" (Proverbs 18:13).

"Seest thou a man that is hasty in his words? There is more hope of a fool than of him" (Proverbs 29:20).

May our ears be open and our mouths ready to speak words of wisdom and encouragement.

Wonderfully Made

We are" *fearfully and wonderfully made"* (Psalms 139:14).

God has designed each of us with a unique personality, enriched us with unique spiritual gifts and placed us in unique life experiences; all for one purpose—to mold and shape us into the likeness of Christ.

During a ladies' retreat several years ago, the speaker shared how she would initiate a conversation with strangers and ultimately share Christ with them. I remember thinking; "I can't do that". The next year, another speaker shared how she gradually built relationships within her neighborhood which over time would result in opportunities to share Christ. I thought; "I can do that". I began to realize "one size doesn't fit all". God uses us as individuals. In my particular case, I am much more comfortable building relationships than speaking up to complete strangers (after all, I have, Bill, my husband who does that).

However, God wants to show Himself strong even in what we label as our limitations.

This was demonstrated to me a short time ago when a plane had some mechanical difficulties, and we sat on the runway for two hours. I decided to work on a PowerPoint for a couple's retreat Bill and I were doing. Soon, I heard a voice from behind me ask, "Are you a missionary?" The man behind me could see my computer screen. Each slide had a Fruit of the Spirit and how that fruit is worked out in the marriage relationship. The man asked me questions regarding each slide. Finally, I asked if there was a time in his life when he accepted Jesus Christ as His Savior [he had]. Now for those of you to whom this would not be a big deal, it was to me. I immediately recognized the event as being orchestrated by God.

My desire is to always to use my gifts and talents to serve Him. At times God takes me out of my comfort zone but I know He uses those times for me to grow and to become more like Jesus Christ.

I still don't go looking for strangers to talk to, but I have confidence in Him, that when given the opportunity, I can do it!

Growing Challenges

Each day God surrounds me with new challenges to cause me to grow. " I wrote this in my devotional journal just a few days before traveling to Washington, DC to see our son-in-law Dan receive the General Douglas McArthur Leadership Award. Dan and Debby are moving back from Germany this summer, so Bill and I decided to bring our grandchildren, Hunter and Sydney, home with us so Dan and Debby can go back and focus on their move.

Dan and Debby drove us to the airport with what we thought was plenty of time to make our flight. But apparently driving 35 miles in less than 2 hours was to be our "new challenge." As we crawled through the heavy DC traffic, I called the airline and found out there was a later flight—but it would cost over $2000 to change all of our tickets. We decided to wait until we got to the airport because it was possible the traffic would lighten up, and we could still make it. However, that was before we ran out of gas…

The GPS showed a gas station .03 miles away. Dan, being a runner, took off for the fuel. I told Hunter; "If Grandma was sleeping, this would be a nightmare." He responded, "If you were sleeping, this wouldn't be happening." To make a long story short – we missed our flight and were put on standby (at no extra cost). We made the next flight with one seat to spare, connected through Detroit, and finally made it home just after midnight.

So it was a tense day, and anxiety tried to rear its ugly head. On a day like that, it's all too easy to dwell on the "if only" scenarios. Of course I had a choice: I could allow my circumstances to rob me of the joy I had just experienced with my family and the excitement of having my grandkids with me; or I could recognize God's grace and "roll with the punches".

"No temptation has overtaken you except such as is common to man; but God is faithful, who will not allow you to be tempted beyond what you are able, but with the temptation will also make the way of escape, that you may be able to bear it" (1 Corinthians 10:13).

We are all tempted to worry; but we must make the decision not based on feelings or circumstances, but on our knowledge of God— and His way of escape.

Tired of it or just plain tired?

Fatigue otherwise known as exhaustion, tiredness, weariness, low or no energy, and weakness affects us physically and emotionally.

Having spent the last three months with grandchildren, working on our cabin in Montana and then helping Dan and Debby move into their new home in Oklahoma (one week after their youngest, Lexus, was born), I can attest to how it feels to lay my head on the pillow exhausted.

Many times physical fatigue is a by-product of emotional fatigue. Anyone who has sat at the bedside of a sick family member or spent hours supporting them as they go through Chemo knows what I am talking about. Not only are you emotionally drained, but physically zapped as well.

We can also become weary in well doing. Bill has always said: "It is no more spiritual to wear out for the Lord than it is to burn out for the Lord." "Keep your priorities right and there is time for everything." "Work hard, then play hard and make no apologies for it." "Sometimes one of the most spiritual things you can do is take a nap." King David did this when he was running for his life and he lay down and slept *(Psalms 3)*. Just getting away for a few hours can refresh us; whether we lie down and sleep or go for a walk.

> *"To everything there is a season, a time for every purpose under heaven"* (Ecclesiastic 3:1).

> *"Seek ye first the kingdom of God and His righteousness, and all these things shall be added to you"* (Matthew 6:33).

We need to guard against over commitment. Even good and godly pursuits must be weighed in light of the purposes of God. We must learn to say no, determine to slow your frantic pace, resist the temptation to add more and more to your schedule. Busyness is not necessarily godliness.

Ask God to help you reprioritize responsibilities. *"For I do always those things that please him"* (John 8:29). *"I have glorified thee on the earth: I have finished the work which thou gavest me to do"* (John 17:4).

Life is Not a Mathematical Equation

Like many good mothers, I told my children God punishes disobedience. Noble teaching…or so I thought until one day while getting into the car our son, Cliff, who was 3 at the time, bumped his head. With teary eyes he quickly exclaimed; "but I didn't do anything wrong."

I was reminded of this last month while in Oklahoma with my daughter and family. I had purchased a small beanbag chair for the kids' room. Sydney discovered that if she ran and jumped on the chair, it would slide across the room. Great fun, except she wanted to do it during Bible reading before bed. You guessed it; she jumped, tumbled and hit her mouth on the floor. Hunter's first response was "that's what she gets for disobeying."

The response of Job's friends was similar. Their conclusion was based on a simple equation: he must have sinned for so many bad things to have happened to him.

It was wrong for Job's friends to make that assumption; but it was not wrong for Job to examine his life. *"How many are mine iniquities and sins? Make me to know my transgression and my sin"* (Job 13:33).

- Our first response to trials should be self-examination—what is God trying to say—did I sin—is my faith lacking? *"Your iniquities have turned away these things, and your sins have withholden good things from you"* (Jeremiah 5:25).

- Our second response should then be*: "Count it all joy. . .* (James 1:2). *"For the LORD God is a sun and shield: the LORD will give grace and glory: no good thing will he withhold from them that walk uprightly"* (Psalms 84:11).

"And we know that all things work together for good to them that love God, to them who are the called according to his purpose" (Romans 8:28).

May we, through times we do not understand, remain faithful and trusting; completely dependent on Him

Falling Stars

While in Montana working on the cabin in late July and early August, we dry camp in my parent's RV. Not quite roughing it but still enjoying the benefits of camping: cooking over the fire, using a port-a-potty, eating while listening to the pitter patter of rain drops on the awning, watching wildlife grazing nearby, sitting by the fire in the morning and evening and waking up in 30 degree temperatures [Bill says 27 if you sleep outside-to which I say; "no thanks"].

However, the greatest of all is watching the stars in the clear Montana sky. After the sun sets, you see one, then another and another. Before long they are too numerous to count, and the "Big Sky" is a display of the Majesty of God.

His Word tells us *"God counts the number of the stars and calls them by name"* (Psalms 147:4). *"They were created through Him and for Him and in Him they consist"* (Colossians 1:16, 17).

This truth baffles my mind as I gaze up at the millions of stars realizing there are billions I cannot even see.

How much more, being created in His likeness, are we valued?

> *"When I consider Your heavens, the work of Your fingers, the moon and the stars, which You have ordained, What is man that You are mindful of him, And the son of man that You visit him? For You have made him a little lower than the angels, And You have crowned him with glory and honor"* (Psalms 8:3-5).

He created our *"inmost being"* (Psalms 139:13) and all *"our days are ordained"* (Psalms 139:16).

He knows our joys, frustrations, hurts and desires, *"For in Him we live, and move, and have our being"* (Acts 17:28).

He has one purpose for us *". . . to be conformed to the image of Jesus Christ"* (Romans 8:29); *"to be changed into the same image from glory to glory"* (2 Corinthians 3:18).

If I stare skyward long enough, I will eventually see a falling star. At times, God allows us to "fall"-- to yield to our frustrations and hurts allowing them to affect us in a negative way. The old nature still raises its ugly head; but God's plan for us never changes.

When we 'fall', let's pick ourselves back up, confess our failure to God and then go forward with confidence knowing *"that he which hath begun a good work in you will perform it until the day of Jesus Christ"* (Philippians 1:6).

Only You Can Prevent Forest Fires

"Even so the tongue is a little member and boasts great things. See how great a forest a little fire kindles! And the tongue is a fire, a world of iniquity. The tongue is so set among our members that it defiles the whole body, and sets on fire the course of nature; and it is set on fire by hell (James 3:4,5).

I remember driving through Yellowstone National Park the summer after a great fire swept over thousands of acres and destroyed everything in its path. As far as your eyes could see, black charred trees covered the landscape. Several years later, during another drive through the park, we saw plant life had returned to the forest floor. But looking closer, we could still see the old burnt stumps scattered among the new trees reminding us of the devastating fire.

Like a fire, words can hurt and destroy. Even after things have been made right, there will always be the ugly stumps which can draw our minds back to the original hurt.

When we need to speak words of correction or rebuke, we need to season our words with grace. The words we speak should bring healing not hurt, restoration not rejection, a positive decision not destruction, and they need to bring about a change in the life of the one confronted.

We also need to be careful when we, ourselves, are burned with hurtful words. Our tendency could be to respond in like, however, God gives us a command:

> *"Let no corrupt word proceed out of your mouth, but what is good for necessary edification, that it may impart grace to the hearers. . . Let all bitterness, wrath, anger, clamor, and evil speaking be put away from you, with all malice* (Ephesians 4:29,31) BUT " *be kind to one another, tenderhearted, forgiving one another, even as God in Christ forgave you"* (Ephesians 4:32). *"Let your speech always be with grace, seasoned with salt, that you may know how you ought to answer each one"* (Colossians 4:6).

May the words of our mouth be acceptable in the sight of God and our Savior Jesus Christ.

Sweet Hour of Prayer

Early in my Christian life, prayer was talking with God and asking Him for things. My growth in the Lord has also resulted in increased knowledge of prayer; not that I will ever fully understand it. Multiple sermons have been preached on the importance of prayer, the requirements for prayer, the pattern for prayer, and the times to pray. Yet, in my life, it is the trials which drive me to my knees, and prayer becomes an intimate part of my life.

While serving as Cliff's (our son was diagnosed with incurable cancer in 2004) care giver, I remember sitting day after day trying to find the right combination of persistence and faith so my prayers would be effective. I was seeking the face of God and wanting the power of God to make things right. He didn't heal Cliff, but He lifted the unbearable weight and gave me peace.

Years ago, I heard an illustration: imagine opening a closet and putting your burden on the shelf; now close the door and leave it there.

> "What a friend we have in Jesus; All our sins and grief to bear! What a privilege to carry everything to God in prayer. O what peace we often forfeit, O what needless pain we bear, all because we do not carry everything to God in prayer."

We see life from a limited view point. The Lord knows how our circumstances fit into His plan. It's not about us--it's about HIM. We are linking our life with the omnipotent power of God not necessarily to do what we want, but for us to want what He wants. He desires to provide for our total well-being: spiritually, physically and materially. *"Beloved, I wish above all things that thou mayest prosper and be in health, even as thy soul prospereth"* (3 John 2).

As you are faced with challenges, hurts or the unknown—pray and seek the face of God; place your burden in the closet and close the door. He will lift the weight, and you will know peace. *"Peace I leave with you, my peace I give unto you: not as the world giveth ...Let not your heart be troubled..."* (John 14:27).

"Sweet hour of prayer, sweet hour of prayer, that calls me from a world of care. . ."

A Mother's Tribute

It was the Thursday before our son, Cliff, died, and we were in the emergency room at Brigham and Women's Hospital in Boston. Cliff said to me "Mom, we always knew one day this was going to happen" to which I replied; "Yes, but it was always in the future." He quietly responded; "This is the future." I turned away not wanting to look at him lying there so tired and weak. Up to this point there had always been a plan; something to try, but now there were no options…the future had arrived.

Cliff and Megan never focused on his cancer or his physical limitations. Yet the realization of them motivated Cliff to work diligently for the Lord. Those who spend day after day with him testify to his knowledge of the Scripture and his zeal for God. He did not complain but used God's gift of cancer to bring Glory to Christ.

> "He explained that our goal as Christians should be to be more like Christ. He used his cancer as an example. He said that his goal shouldn't be to get rid of his cancer, if it went away that's great.... but his goal was to use his cancer to be more like Christ."   Student Nate Gaudet

"A good name is better than precious ointment, and the day of death than the day of birth" (Ecclesiastics 7:1). I gave birth to Cliff, and it was a wonderful day; but God says the day of his death was better.

As a mother, I want the very best for my children. On April 1, 2011, Cliff received the very best God has to offer. *"In my Father's house are many mansions . . . I go to prepare a place for you. And if I go and prepare a place for you, I will come again, and receive you unto myself; that where I am, there ye may be also"* (John 14:2-3).

I look forward to the day we will be reunited and together we will be with the Lord forever. In the meantime I want to follow in my son's footsteps and focus on God's goodness in my life regardless of the circumstances.

He Lives

This past Sunday, while singing *He Lives* ♫, I was struck by the truth of these words in my life during the past few months:

> ♪ *I see His hand of mercy, I hear His voice of cheer, and just the time I need Him, He's always near.*♫ The song goes on; ♪*"In all the world around me I see His loving care, and tho' my heart grows weary, I never will despair, I know that He is leading thro' all the stormy blast* (and praise God) *the day of His appearing will come at last. ♪ He lives, He lives! ♪ Christ Jesus lives today! He walks with me and talks with me along life's narrow way. ♪ He lives, He lives, salvation to impart! You ask me how I know He lives? He lives within my heart."* ♪♫

What an expression of my life's verse *"I am crucified with Christ: nevertheless I live; yet not I, but Christ liveth in me: and the life which I now live in the flesh I live by the faith of the Son of God, who loved me, and gave himself for me"* (Galatians 2:20).

I certainly do serve a risen Savior! My God is not dead! Because of this I can sing: ♪ *Rejoice, rejoice O Christian, lift up your voice and sing. Eternal hallelujahs to Jesus Christ, the King! The Hope of all who seek Him, the Help of all who find, None other is so loving, so good and kind.* ♫

I have heard people ask; "how can a loving God allow terrible things to happen?"

The truth is: God is loving, God is good, God is kind, yet God does allow things in our life which can cause us to grow weary.

It is during those times I have the opportunity to recognize who God is and desire to know Him more intimately because I know He is not only the light at the end of the tunnel, but the He is the Light in the tunnel.

Knowing this, can you lift your voices with me and sing;

♫ Hallelujah to Jesus Christ, the King!

A Battle for the Mind

Our trip back to Dublin Christian Academy in May for their high school graduation was in some ways a difficult time. This was where Cliff lived for the last 10 years and where I cared for him for six months nearly seven years ago.

At the end of the festivities, driving away from campus was hard. Although Cliff was no longer physically there, it was still a connection to him.

Our home in Michigan is not his childhood home. Sometimes I wished it were so I could go in his room and sit. I do not want his voice, his smile, the feel of his hand to fade from my memory.

A battle rages in my mind. I know the scripture, but at times, I think it unfair. I know God's best has been accomplished, but it wasn't what I would have chosen. I want him here to live a happy life with Megan, but I know without a doubt that he is happier than he ever could be. You see how my mind battles back and forth.

I thought of Eve in the garden when Satan said;

"Has God indeed said" (Genesis 3:1).

I criticize her for her lack of faith, yet I find myself hearing those words.

While in NH, I read Cliff's journals from two of his summer ministries: Trail's End Ranch in Montana and teaching in China. How wise my son was becoming then. He desired to serve God, yet there were times he said his selfishness would raise its ugly head. He wrote about needing peace not daily, but moment by moment seeking God's presence. And as he saw God answer, his response was "God is good".

Yes, we all know God's way is best. But at times what our mind knows and what our heart feels don't match. We must FOCUS on the truth; have FAITH in a just God and as my husband says: "your feelings will follow."

"Therefore my heart is glad, and my glory rejoices;
My flesh also will rest in hope" (Psalms 16:9).

Jesus, the Sweetest Name

There are numerous reasons a name is chosen: a family name passed down through generations, a name in honor of a loved one, a popular name, a unique name or a name with a special meaning. A name can be chosen (or rejected) simply because of what or who it represents.

- The name Jesus was chosen by God.

"the angel said unto her. . .thou shalt conceive in thy womb, and bring forth a son, and shalt call his name JESUS" (Luke 1:30-31).

- God knew who the child would be and what the child would do.

"And she shall bring forth a son, and thou shalt call his name JESUS: for he shall save his people from their sins" (Matthew 1:20-21).

- There is power in the name JESUS!

". . . by the name of Jesus Christ of Nazareth, . . . there is none other name under heaven given among men, whereby we must be saved" (Acts 4:10-12).

"Peter said . . . In the name of Jesus Christ of Nazareth rise up and walk" (Acts 3:6).

"But Paul . . . said to the spirit, I command thee in the name of Jesus Christ to come out of her" (Acts 16:18).

". . . he had preached boldly at Damascus in the name of Jesus" (Acts 9:27).

"That at the name of Jesus every knee should bow, of things in heaven, and things in earth, and things under the earth" (Philippians 2:10).

> ♫ "Jesus is the sweetest name I know,
>
> And He's just the same as His lovely name.
>
> And that's the reason why I love Him so;
>
> Jesus is the sweetest name I know." ♫

As we speak the name of Jesus, may we focus on how **that name** has changed us and live accordingly.

Made in the USA
Monee, IL
30 June 2020